Also by Lucia Blinn:

Passing For Normal
Navigating The Night
We Called It "The Country"
Celadon
Memo To Marty
Sounds Like Lucia (CD)

Sonoma

Poems

Lucia Blinn

LINDA —
ENJOY YOUR STAY IN
SONOMA,
Lucia

Sonoma
Poems by Lucia Blinn

ISBN# 978-1-887229-45-6

Published by First Flight Books
A division of Bruce Bendinger Creative Communications, Inc.
2144 N. Hudson • Chicago, IL 60614
773-871-1179 • FX 773-281-4643
www.firstflightbooks.com

FIRST FLIGHT BOOKS

Book Deisgn: Meredith Blinn
Cover Design: Gregory S. Paus

For further information, you may e-mail the author:
luciablinn@gmail.com.

To Meredith & Daphne & Achiya
with my love

Contents

You Should be a Copywriter

Summer, high school junior year, Detroit.
I needed a more solid job than hustling goods
and services for Welcome Wagon.
Ever enrolled in the school of serendipity,
I drove around the neighborhood and stopped
at a neatly-landscaped pharmaceutical firm.
As their newest employee, assistant to the advertising
manager, I typed and filed stencils for flyers
for the drugs they sold—as tedious as it sounds.

At some point, the manager said:
You should be a copywriter.
What had he heard from me that would elicit
that statement? Having no idea what copywriter
meant, I looked it up: one who writes copy. Oh.
The following year, I answered an ad for another
summer job, this one at BBDO, Jack Benny's agency.
Could I type? asked the office manager.
Did hunt and peck count?

I lied, taught myself to type in one feverish day,
stuffing my wastebasket and the ladies'
room's and sneaking home even more typo'd
paper (the writer had said No Erasures).
I was up till the small hours but I figured it out
and was soon turning in typo-free copy.
Two weeks later, I complained that I was bored.
Do you want to write a commercial?

And thus commenced the fiesta of my life.
I left the sticks of Detroit for the mighty majesty
of Madison Avenue. I was nineteen
and newly launched on a thirty-year
advertising career in New York and Chicago.
My fellow writers were clever and funny
and I was their wide-eyed altar girl.
The pay was too good and too much of it
was funneled into designer boutiques.
Neurotic spending, drinking and writing ads
were the drill.

Spending and drinking have since sobered;
typing—commercials for me, of a sort—
continues to sustain me.

I Gave at the Office

The deal was: donate a day's wages
to the Crusade of Mercy fund drive
and be eligible to win a trip for two to Paris.
I dutifully donated then mused about
how nifty it would be to win.
And I did.
Only to be subjected to a year of taunts
from bad-sport colleagues who groused:
Of all the people who didn't need to win.

You can't judge a copywriter by her cover.
They had been taken in by my looking the part
of someone trailing a trust fund,
courtesy of a pear-shaped diamond,
designer clothes and an Attitude.
The reality was I was no more solvent
than the next ink-stained wretch
and required regular infusions of income
to keep my act intact.
Where *is* that trust fund?

Ad Dreams

They happen rarely now. Thirty years later,
a statute of limitations.
Still there was I, back at the Agency last night
dreaming an advertising dream with tall, dreamy,
account guy, Dick Stanwood.
It felt right and safe being employed again
with all those whip-smart writers and art directors.
We were always laughing. Life in the trenches
with millions on the line, not as terrifying as today.
Or was it the padded buffer of garden-variety
youth and martinis that created the illusion?
(*Make 'em doubles and keep 'em coming.*
- a legendary drunk)
As for the actual work of writing commercials,
who imagined it was an internship for the verses
I scribble today?

Off to Work

I left the office decades ago
but the office never left me.
I still need to get out to get
these poems out.
Stay home at my white desk
over the blue bay and green park?
No.
Home is laundry, cooking, email,
gardening, MSNBC, bubble-bathing
and reading.
So I pack my Mac, cross the street
and hope no one's in my corner
at the coffee shop so I can work
so I can play.
Never stop working. - Marc Chagall

Resumé

Summing up a career in seventeen words:

Wrote commercials in New York
& Chicago for major clients;
paid well to wrangle with clever people.

Back stories (1955 – 1987)

*Wrote commercials at BBDO-NY
for Campbell Soup & Lucky Strike
with hat-in-the-office Margery Fowler

*Wrote commercials for Revlon, Clairol
& Chanel at NCK-NY with legendary
Norman B. Norman & Kay Daly

*Wrote commercials for Marshall Field's
& Brownberry Ovens at K&E-Chicago
with artist Tom Sasser

*Wrote commercials for Kellogg's & Campbell's
at Leo Burnett-Chicago with legendary Leo

*Wrote commercials for General Mills, Kraft,
& S.C. Johnson at DDB-Chicago with legendary
Keith Reinhard

It was a thirty-year war.
Hindsight: had I worked in boutiques
rather than behemoth agencies,
my best campaigns would have survived.
(See "Adtopsy" in my book,
We Called It 'The Country')

Memo from the
Bleak End of 2016

H.L. Mencken, that knew-it-all,
has the first word:

*As democracy is perfected, the office of president
represents, more and more closely, the inner soul of
the people. On some great and glorious day, the plain
folks of the land will reach their hearts' desire at last,
and the White House will be adorned by a downright
moron.*

It was midnight in America.
The clock struck twelve
and we all turned into pumpkins.
The end of the world as we knew it
happened on 11/8...the new 9/11.

After a brutal campaign of unprecedented vitriol—we
moaned and groaned of little else—it was Election Day.
Those who bought the snake oil and those who chose
to hate Hillary voted not for the most qualified
candidate in modern history but for the least qualified.

Rather than an informed woman of discipline,
they elevated Twitterman, an inarticulate,
vulgar, sexual predator and bully.
Psychiatry tells us he suffers from a Narcissistic
Personality Disorder wherein he abhors rules and
traditions, is manifestly defiant, abrasive, craves
adulation, and scorns information:
I know more than the generals.

He never imagined actually winning,
but up at the podiums with Little Marco,
low-energy Jeb, and crooked Hillary,
as he mocked them, and who hinted
that Cruz Sr. had a hand in doing in JFK,
never mind sticks and stones,
his name-calling more than hurt them;
he ate their lunch, breakfast and dinner.
He had help. After Putin hammered a few
nails in Clinton's coffin, Comey dug her a grave.

The ignominious head of the Divided States
of America is a man of cons and conflicts
whose DNA is hard-core chutzpah;
a liar to make Pinocchio blush,
who wouldn't know decorum if it plopped him
on his pompadour, and who has plunged us
into global humiliation.
The German paper, *Der Spiegel,* called him
the most dangerous man in the world.
He is a loose cannon in a nuclear china shop.
NYT's Paul Krugman predicted that this
will be worse than we can possibly imagine.

Sanity has left the building.
Half the country is sitting shivah
disbelieving, appalled, terrified.

Let it be known I tried to save us.
When the Cubs were World Series-bound,
I offered the Almighty a deal:
I'd give up the Cubs if He'd give us Hillary.
He was game till Game 7
when He pulled that rain stunt.
Who knew God was a Cubs fan?

We are now dealing with Fake News.
It's a real head-shaker because fiction has
a tough time being stranger than today's
news of craziness which sounds too surreal
to be real which makes it hard to know
what to believe, and all of it makes one sad
and weary which argues for tuning it out
and hopping into bed with Jeeves.

America will not be destroyed from the outside.
If we falter and lose our freedoms,
it will be because we have destroyed ourselves.
                              - Abraham Lincoln

In Their Fashion

Do you remember when a woman wore
a tent to conceal her pregnancy?
I recall the day I came face-to-tummy
with the new look.
At the office before the birth of her twins,
Nancy Jordan appeared in a tight bright orange
sweater that left no doubt about her state.
It must have been okay to stare because
it was impossible to ignore that looming sphere.
Nancy was a pioneer fashionista so you knew
that flaunting baby was the thing.

As the world spins ever more dizzyingly,
we pause to note that once upon a quaint era,
women were slaves to skirt length.
We bowed way down to Dior's mid-calf New Look
and chopped off acres for the mini-look.
There was a costly ivory linen number I cut
up to here only to realize I looked ridiculous.
Age does indeed have its privileges.
As today's young lemmings parade
in micro-shorts, piercings, tattoos, green hair
and dresses that look like nightgowns,
I pull on my khakis and tees and give thanks.

Memo to TV Anchors

This little rant is about what you
or your stylists deem appropriate
for appearing in our living rooms.
A shallow issue? We are nothing
if not shallow, your viewers.
Look. The news is not a fashion show
and you are not on a runway.
Please. Rethink the baubles, beads,
scarves (don't leave home with them)
and tops of every stripe, print, plaid,
floral and shrieking neon.
These do not a vision of gravitas make.
Consider muted fabrics that do not
distract and detract from your message.
Find a low-key look that works for your work,
i.e., the brilliant Rachel who simply slips
into a dark jacket, and Bob's your uncle.
Please. We're up to here in Issues without
having to deconstruct your fashion statements.

Into the Closet

There is no knowing about fashion.
No knowing which pieces that wink
with promise in the shops might rarely,
if ever, come out of the closet or which
will see you into a movie, a meeting,
or moonlight cruise and become
an indispensable friend. Speaking of.
No telling with friends, either.
No predicting what separates the ephemeral
fair-weather chaff from the rocky roads
of till-death-do-you-part wheat.
Whatever happened to whatshername?

Three Bags Empty

There they sit high on a shelf in my closet
in all their bamboo-handled glory—a trio
of Gucci handbags, props from another stage.
Black, camel and the late Irma's white
I saw first at her feet in Toni Robin's office
on Madison Avenue.
The things they carried, these treasures
($90 then, $2,200 now) in the simpler sixties:
keys, comb, cash, lipstick, handkerchief.
Unimaginable that one day I couldn't navigate
without an iPhone, iPad, cache of cosmetics
and credit cards, silk scarf, thin socks, ball cap,
sunglasses, distance and reading glasses,
hearing aid batteries, pens and paper,
and an iced latté.

It's all gotten exponentially complex, this business
of getting and spending and laying waste our powers,
as Wordsworth's words put it.
And whatever for besides our one true pursuit:
booking passage on the River Styx.
Just saying.

Stalking Joan Didion

There is a resemblance.
People called to ask if it were I
in a Joan Didion ad for Celine.
And there is a bond.
I am drawn to her lapidary prose
and past life with John Donne;
they never ran out of conversation.
She was mixing a salad minutes
before he died.
(She said mixing, not tossing.)
I have a worn Vogue article with photos
of their New York apartment.
I have read her raw tales of loss—
John and daughter Quintana Roo
(named for a federal entity in Mexico).
I tracked down an elusive tote bearing an image
of a brooding Joan with a cigarette.
And bought a book about authors,
a lean, smoking Joan leans on its cover.
She said she just writes about what's interesting.
That would be you, Ms. Didion.
In a moment of precocious prescience,
I named my doll for you and for my baby
chose your name for Meredith's middle.
I continue as acolyte to your muse.

What is This?

I call it a poem.
The stickler professor and others
of his ilk, balk.
Really?
I can't take the time to rhyme?
Sticklers might be advised
that poems went into free fall,
i.e., non-rhyming eons ago.
Permission, therefore, granted my verses
that sometimes include an inside rhyme.
Otherwise, note the for-the-most-part
narrow lines that look like and read like
a poem or at least vertical tales.
If the esteemed, enigmatic *New Yorker*
pieces parade as poetry...

I Can't Read This

...this being a note I scribbled to myself
some days ago. Something worth noting
or something needing action; however, my writing
has devolved from what might have passed
for interesting into hieroglyphics full of swirls
and flourishes signifying nothing.
This memo, among others, suggests rust
in the motor skill sector pointing to the need
to p-r-i-n-t which involves s-l-o-w-i-n-g down
and begs the question:
What's the rush to enter Valhallah?

Our wise Buddhist, Paul, cautions:
Time swiftly passes by and opportunity is lost.
Each of us should strive to awaken, awaken.
Take heed; do not squander your life.

Good Question

In the midst of my poetry reading
at a retirement home, a man asked
Are you Jewish?
Yes, I'm a convert.
At the end of the reading, he asked
Were you always this funny,
or just since you've been Jewish?

Dying to Spend

What compelled them to shop
after a diagnosis of terminal cancer?
Irma told of sailing right into Bergdorf
and arming herself with a pile of cashmere
sweaters in shades of coffee and mocha
that played to her keen brown eyes.
Then into Pierre Deux for fifty yards
of raspberry-and-cream toile to re-do
her boudoir.
We'd shared a long friendship, this New York
glamour girl and I. Long chats in her Wedgwood
living room and long lunches in west-side bistros,
she in her head-turning hats.
We never tired of grousing about politics,
Irma mystified by everyone's kindness to Reagan.
I feasted on her pale blue letters telling
of weekends in Newtown (!) where she harvested
lilies for her Manhattan flat.

As for Marty who lived thirty years
into our marriage, shopping was an ingrained
response; he had been born a clotheshorse
with the looks that went with it.
He chose modestly the bleak afternoon after
the gastroenterologist delivered the bleak news:
metastasized pancreatic cancer.
Two pairs of Bermudas for the country,
two pairs for the city.
Marty lived an unexpected two more years,
his jackets dwarfing his diminishing frame.

It's been twenty-five years.
Our life together seems a vintage movie.
Metacritic would have given it a 70.

Sonoma

Consider the clout of a cardboard box
at the café where I had settled in with
a mid-winter's poem.
Below an illustration of grapevines:
Grand Cru Vineyards 2016 Pinot Noir
Sonoma, California
And that's all it took to take me away
from my words about the bird I heard
to the B&B amid the vineyards of Sonoma—
our last holiday as a family.
At a drugstore nearby, the tabloid blared:
3 Months To Live!
Michael Landon dying of pancreatic cancer!
The very scourge that Marty was living with
and dying from.

After ravishing days that began with our host's
signature strawberry pancakes, we toured wineries,
creeped out in tubs of sludge at Calistoga
and marveled at the fare in gorgeous restaurants.
They live with fire and earthquake, but Californians
own the franchise of exquisite fresh food.

There was a bittersweet evening of farewell
with Marty's brother who had been detached.
Since the cancer, he had re-striped himself
as solicitous and later turned on me after I naively
sent him my first book that held nothing back.
To the living we owe kindness;
to the dead we owe the truth. - Voltaire

On our last night, beneath the winking stars
of a midnight sky, the girls and I reveled in a
soothing hot tub and told tales of other trips,
even as we batted away the looming shadow
of loss.

Lulu & Poppy

Long before it could even happen,
I gave us grandparent names—Lulu & Poppy.
Never mind that he balked at being named
for a flower; he wouldn't live to object.
Never mind that I would be 0 for 2
in the granny game.
Never mind that we never made it
to our eponymous islands: St Lucia & St. Martin.
Or to the place he'd sort of lusted after—
New Zealand.
Or that I'd rather hoped to roam around
the rhinos in Kenya.
And see what Machu Picchu was all about.
Or tuck into that flat in Florence again.

Travel has become travail, i.e., my recent
6 flights in 10 days to 3 states.
It took resetting my trapezoids or traps,
as the acupuncturist called them, to stop hurting.
All that sitting, she said, and lugging stuff.
So, what now, voyager?
Wasn't it I who, lo those whirly twirly years ago,
yearned for the peace to pursue long walks
and long books?
Pascal reminds us:
*Most of our troubles are attributable to our refusal
to sit quietly in our rooms.*

Sport & Fifi

Their names might have been Mary & Bob,
but my mother, acerbic beneath her prim manner,
noting the woman's fuzzy blond hair
and her husband's thin quick steps,
privately dubbed the new neighbors
Sport & Fifi.
No more than Hello passed over the fence,
mom not given to chatting.

I was home for her funeral and outside
with my sister, Martha, when the blond
came out. Not in on the joke, Martha said,
Hello, Fifi.
What did you call me?
My sister is confused, I said, *our mom just died.*
Oh, I'm sorry. She was so nice.

Martin Stuart Blinn 1931 – 1993

His was a noteworthy resumé.
Marty knew so many composers,
he could have won a jackpot.
His voice was so rich and romantic,
he might have sung for the world.
There was hardly a dog he didn't know;
he could have judged the Westminster.
His Ivy League passion ran so deep,
he could have been a Brooks Brother.

Marty instead was Lucia's loving ballast,
Meredith's soulmate, Daphne's snappy foil,
staunch ally of Bruce & Pam, Tina & Pete;
ardent friend and gifted teller
of Abe & Sam & Becky tales.
Marty was a master in the kitchen:
tuna with white pepper, take it or leave it.
He always ordered the best dessert
then had to put up with our sharing.
A virtuoso of the tie and brass buckle,
he kept a car like a piece of art.
And he was always there for us.
Hi Kid, he'd say and you could wrap yourself
in the love that spoke.

Marty is singing again and fishing
and golfing and swimming and soaring.
We hear the laughter. We smile back.

The Brain that Couldn't

Mrs. Kerwin really really tried but it's doubtful
anyone could have pried the notes off the page
and into my head and fingers to make music.
Pity my math-teacher brother, Muntz,
who tried and tried and failed to crack open
my cranium and pour in even a modest number
of numbers of the algebraic persuasion.
And Rick, the banker who periodically
deciphered the chaos in my checkbook
until darling Meredith, who never met
an Augean Stable she wasn't determined
to demolish, took over.
A woolgatherer who wanders in the woods
in search of an ever-absent left brain is left
with no choice but to write her head off.

Life begins the day you start a garden.
                    - Chinese proverb

In Search of My Mother's Garden

Mom tended an old-fashioned garden.
She didn't talk or fuss about it; working
in her garden was just what she did.
Nor did she bring flowers into the house
though she might have arranged plenty
of peonies, roses, daisies and tiger lilies.

Her seeds spouted in my soul.
I rode my bicycle to a ramshackle greenhouse
with grimy broken windows and sad plants
withering on shabby tables.
The owner, a frumpy lump of a woman, rumored
to be the spouse of Old Nick, the ice cream man,
indulged my shy presence:
You can play with anything that's dead.

Years later, I picked up Mom's trowel and began
gardening at our little red house in the country
with its white lilacs, blue irises, pale peonies
and trusty orange daylilies.
We added hundreds of daffodils and tulips—
Queen of Shebas and black and white Parrots
and harvested buckets of them for the city.

I have long since treasured the pleasure
of browsing nurseries, a spiritual experience.
Having moved to a vintage building after a trip
to Provence, I mounted window boxes filled
with salmon geraniums and periwinkle petunias.
In a contemporary building, I lavished its balconies
with dozens of pots of annuals and willow branches
climbing with morning glories and moonflowers
that glowed in the dark.

In my current home overlooking Sarasota Bay,
my garden is a baker's rack adorned with trailing
English and Algerian ivy and Bromeliads.
Much like the country flowers that had to rouse
themselves for my Friday night inspections by flashlight
(*Oh dear, she's back*), these are subject to
early morning perusal.
Somewhere amid a rosy field of waving cosmos,
Mom smiles.

If you have a library and a garden, you have all you need.
                                        - Cicero

*...when to be young was
very heaven.*   - William Wordsworth

I'll go with summer mornings
when I was very young.
Grade school was out.
(We didn't call it middle school.)
The gentle warmth of early June.
The mild breeze and innocence
of untrammeled hours.
Sudden summer rains.
We ran outside to rescue sheets
drying on the line.
Rarely hot, never cold.
No calendars, no phones, nothing
but bicycles and Monopoly, listening
to *Let's Pretend* on Sharon's screened porch,
and, sweetest of all, reading in the quiet green
of the backyard.
Wasn't it something, the fleeting softness
and safety of those golden, olden days?

Mink

My father's friend, Jack Preston,
owned a mink farm somewhere
in the green hills of Pennsylvania.
I recall seeing the squirmy silky brown
things in their cages up on stilts.
Connect them to the coats I would covet
and ultimately turn my back on?
$8,000 to parade in the plush pelts
of the dead? Oh, please.

The beautiful and brainy Carol K. had multiple
furs, an enviable marriage, friends, family
and fortune and a life of strife at sixty.
When she became disabled with ALS, her
husband designed a mink blanket for her wheelchair
and continued to lavish her with luxury—
wheeling her into Cartier for jewels
and into Saks for Rykiel sweaters.
His pursuit of esoteric treatment kept her alive
for her goal: a grandson's bar mitzvah.
Carol by then was alive by the thinnest definition;
she was immobile as marble.
One hopes the mink helped.

Sundays at the Janiks'

A precocious older sister—the one who saved
my life by pouring a bucket of diaper water
over baby me who had turned blue—
that quick-thinker named me Lucia
as in di Lammermoor, giving me license
for a time to pass as Italian. Parents born
in Poland, however, what was the point?

Numerous relatives settled in Hamtramck,
the Polish enclave adjacent to Detroit—
some of them being the Janiks.
You might pronounce their name like J
as in jam but, being Polish, it's Y as in yam.

Sundays meant visiting them which meant
Pinochle and highballs for the men,
crocheting for the women, hide-and-seek
with cousins Patsy, Camille and glamorous Gwennie
and Margo; and for supper, Daddy's famed kielbasa
on the oil-cloth-covered kitchen table.
After which anyone not playing cards gathered
on the front porch to talk about absent relatives
till it was dark and time to go home, noting
the usual lighted landmarks without a thought
about how many more or fewer times
I'd see them out the window of the car.

Malling

The first mall I recall was in the fifties.
A shopping mall, whatever that meant,
was opening on a vast piece of real estate
in Detroit. Its name was Eastland
and what it meant was that many shops
were opening in one place—the beginning
of the human swarm that soon took over the land.
Prior to this, you went downtown to Hudson's
or Crowley's or to a neighborhood mom-and-pop
shop for shoes, now mall'd out of business.

Lots of landlords today make lots of loot
on these glittering sprawls, including a cousin
who lives a grand life in grand houses.
Last week, at Neiman's in a mall in Delray Beach,
a teeny terrier trapped in a Burberry carrier
yapped its unhappiness causing its stiletto-heeled
mistress holding a $2,000 jacket to shake the bag
and hiss: *Stop it!*
So many stores, so many stories.

The Brevoort

A grand old grey building, The Brevoort
on lower Fifth Avenue was a subway ride
from my office on Madison Avenue.
I made the trip three noons a week
to the humorless analyst.
Don't you think that's funny? I asked
about an observation.
There's nothing funny here, he answered.
Had I been of stronger stuff, I'd have gotten
up and out, but I wasn't so I didn't.
No telling what if anything of note sifted
into my murky twenty-something psyche.
Seeing a psychiatrist was just what we
of a certain strata did, i.e., my fellow writer
and would-be-romance, Bob, with whom
I exchanged waves across the subway tracks—
he headed uptown to his appointment,
I downtown to mine.

The upside of the whole charade was,
as is often the case for me, lunch.
After my leaden session, I sat beside
manicured matrons in The Brevoort coffee shop
and watched the counterman fix a sandwich
for the calorie-counters.
I studied his slicing toast horizontally
then spreading one side with tuna or egg salad.
No fries.
Was it relief at being off the couch
that rendered it magical?
Proust had his madeleines;
I have my memories:
Mom's potato pancakes.
Hamburgers at the Acorn on Oak.
Chinese at Wing Yee.
Chicken salad and coffee milk shakes
with Daphne after ballet at the Drake.
What gustatory offering merits
remembering today? Pasta? Pesto? Pizza?

Chopped Liver

Not as in, *What am I ...?* but as in Bertie's
celestial offering in the Long Island sunroom
on summer weekends with drinks.
Make that drink. As I made for a refill,
my icy martinet of a father-in-law, Jack,
admonished: *That stuff's intoxicating.*
Well, the weekends were free, complete
with Jack's factotum driving into Manhattan
for us on Friday nights.
The drink preceded a standing rib roast
prepared by Nora, the dour housekeeper.
Don't ask how she is, Bertie warned.
I always forgot and Nora always said,
About the same.
She might have been speaking for her mistress.
The elegant Georgian house that Jack built
for Bertie echoed with her misery.
Other than frequent forays into dusty
thrift shops hunting for treasure, she was ever
the disappointed bride unable to extricate
herself from Jack's chilly disapproval.
Easy on the bread, Bert, he'd say,
effectively raining on her small parade.

I had wishfully imagined that after Jack's death,
Bertie might emerge from her repression
and depression and realize her potential as...what?
An antiques dealer?
She had an unerring eye and impeccable taste.
A talk show host?
She was smart and ironic with no end of gab.
A doting grandmother?
Too broken for that.
Bertie took to her bed and her faulty heart
took it from there, leaving us with a legacy
of material possessions and memories of her wit.

Indelible Inedibles

Three past repasts live on in infamy:
I.
The dinner on Central Park West
at 7:00 in the sixties.
The hosts greeted and seated six of us
in the living room and offered drinks.
Then disappeared.
We watched our watches.
At 7:40, they reappeared
with conversation. Without food. Ever.
We came, we drank, we left.
II.
Meredith invited her classmate, Eva,
and her parents, the German consul and wife
to dinner. An interesting prospect.
A memorable misadventure.
A fork into my trusty roast chicken
proved the unthinkable: it was rare.
How was it I chose to remember Julia Child
advising us to never apologize?
Had I misunderstood?
Ah, to rewind that evening and pop
the blasted bird back in the oven.
And pour more drinks.
III.
Come at 7:00, said the hostess
of the grand Kenilworth manse.
At 7:30, there was wine.
At 8:00, there was celery and brie.
And just as we thought to leave
after 9:00—had we misunderstood?—
we were summoned to the high-ceilinged,
silver-and-crystal-festooned dining room wherein
a uniformed servant served cavernous bowls
of spicy, mud-thick black bean soup.
Followed by bloody steaks.
Followed by profiteroles at 11:00.
If this is the 1%...

The Sex Thing

Some sage said:
There are no secrets; sooner or later,
everyone knows everything.
As the good old boys and their lascivious
fraternity are outed, my own history
is recalled: the sleazy producer who made
an inappropriate suggestion,
the host who kissed me behind
his wife's back, and the outrageous
invitation from a CEO.
They qualified as discomfort, not abuse,
and not that I snitched.
The sorority finally woke up and spoke up
and a serious taboo was blasted as we stagger
toward the obliteration of our culture.
Some say that life is not a rehearsal.
Perhaps this one is just that:
A preview of sorts in which we stumble
and sin and learn the stupid way to make
wrong things right.
All things are possible?
Redemption, anyone?
One sunny day, there may be tickets
for the new and improved, sweet, kind,
flawless and well, yes, a bit boring—Life.
Till then, best hang on.

The Summer of our Despair

My family was far from the first on the block
to own a Television Set, but it wasn't long
before Milton Berle moved in followed in quick
order by my mother's mantra:
Turn that thing down.
Years later, I did her one better.
Can we have that off?
Hearing my key in the lock,
the girls rushed to switch it off.

Hyper fast-forward to this, the summer of '17
where, now living alone (where did they all go?),
I am addicted to the insidious television opera
featuring the shockingly elected charlatan
who has oozed a cancer over our very
foundation, anathema to all that is decent.

The Obamas had to be excised; all that goodness
insufferable, so we got the darkest of flip sides.
Was it our hubris, a sense of superiority
that had to be knocked down?
Now a laughingstock on the world stage,
we are humbled and humiliated.
The NYT's David Brooks wrote of what he
foresaw as this president's death march:
long, slow and ugly.

And from the estimable Philip Roth:
…he is ignorant of government, of history,
of science, of philosophy, of art, incapable of
expressing subtlety or nuance, destitute of all decency,
and wielding a vocabulary of seventy-seven words
that is better called Jerkish than English.
What is most terrifying is that he makes any and
everything possible, including, of course,
the nuclear catastrophe.

No knowing where this blighted road leads.
Will he implode of a heart attack?
His physiology suggests it.
An assassination?
De rigueur at dinner parties:
placing bets on impeachment.
By the time this is in print, our so-called president
may be benighted history.

There are all manner of theories as to
How This Happened.
How did an ignorant racist groper come to sit
at the desk of men who were, for the most part,
humbled by the enormity of their responsibility?
As for the V.P. in the wings, we are warned:
It Could Be Worse.
Long past America The Beautiful.
We are America The Unrecognizable.

Cold Turkey

Announcing a major medical breakthrough
for sufferers of Advanced Newsiosis!
You know the symptom:
You set out for a walk in the park
and rather than hearing birdsong,
a malevolent litany plays in your head:

Department of Justice
Military intervention
Syria
Russia
Special counsel
Impeachment
White house lawyers
Sex
Lies
Leaks
Laundering
Investigation
Resigned
Counter intelligence
Fired
Harassment
Polls
2018
Off-shore
Malignant narcissism
Tax bill
Groping
Collusion
Clinton emails
Fake News
2020

America, relief is at hand.
Introducing Cold Turkey.
Follow these simple direction:
Turn off your TV.
Your misery back if you turn it on.
Caution:
Side effects include restful sleeping.

What I Don't Worry About

Daddy said:
Only crazy people worry about Money.
He didn't, which didn't qualify him as the sanest
butcher whoever put blade to beef,
but the man did sleep soundly.
He also said: *Money in the bank?*
What good is it in there?
He had a point, an idiotic point, as George Sanders
said to Marilyn Monroe about not addressing
the butler as butler.
Do I worry about Dow Jones?
Worst case: Walgreen's is hiring.
And why agonize about World War III?
As the inimitable Maloney opined:
The only thing that's the end of the world
is the end of the world.
Let me not fret over possible decisions
en route to The End. My energy is finite.
True, disaster looms on every front, side and back.
Joan Didion wrote of *the unspeakable peril*
of the everyday.
However. Until the big bad Whatever descends,
I say to the laughing Angel in the ballroom:
Dance with me. I want to be your partner.

Sidewalk Poetry II

"...so we're in this jail cell..."

"...had a heart attack, in the hospital, lives in Iowa..."

"...she actually has 4 kids, 3 from my cousin, 1 from that..."

"... so the doctor said to me..."

"...I didn't realize how good these pants fit until..."

"...what about the $200,000?..."

"...he's had 3 back fusions by a doctor who invented
the machine, and then..."

"...I want you out of this house this week..."

"...No! $35 at the flea market..."

" ...I don't think your sister is speaking to me..."

"...you ready for this?..."

"...unless you beat the hell out of that kid and it's caught
on camera, you're OK..."

"...wait, who is this?"

The Phantom

The elegant author, Nancy, pointed out
the need for a poem about our patrician
friend Pattie's blink-and-you'll-miss him,
freelance, commitment-phobic beau, R.
I've never clapped eyes on the bloke
but why would that stop me from wandering
into the tall weeds and wondering if I could
work my way out of I knew-not-what.

Herewith, an ode to the sort-of-kind-of-
on-again-off-again, now-you-see-him-
now-you-don't, MIA/AWOL, fleet-footed
fellow who wings in and wings out on a whim,
a hale-and-sometimes-met man
with the attention span of a cricket,
an under-the-covers agent who loves her
and leaves her while the pillow's still warm.
A poster boy for a Wanted poster.
His face on a milk carton.
> *Bi-coastal runaway!*
> *Catch this Catch if you can!*

Slippage

One slipped out of Meredith's car.
One slipped out of a pocket in the park.
One slipped down the trash chute.
Is there existential meaning in losing
three pairs of RX glasses in three months?
I have nearly healed the wound of leaving
the plu-perfect scarf in a taxi.
Gone too but for the occasional pang
are the cashmere shawl and diamonds.
The phrase is gone for good;
surely this is gone for bad.
Why is this happening?
- Am I ever more distracted?
- Am I losing my grip on the temporal?
- Has St. Anthony, finder of the lost,
  cut me off?

Having attained advanced age, I continue to lose
friends and family, have hung up the car keys,
and hang on to the traces of yester-youth.

As for gains...
- I am in less of a hurry so as not to sustain
  a fifth bone-breaking fall.
- I am following Ann Patchett's year of not spending:
  fun & profit.
- I no longer host elaborate dinners.
- I have learned to nap.

A death

Note the small d, no one has actually died;
rather the end of our seventeen-year run.
I shipped the rest of your things
three-thousand miles west.
Tossed the remains of your beloved
blue cheese dressing, marinara Ragú and
cardboard container of ground cardboard—
Kraft Parmesan.
I see you not here in your chair.
I see me alone with me after all your scary
surgeries and the awful cruise that broke
my bones; all the movies and dinner parties
with the good friends you came with,
your sardonic humor, and let me count
the ways we disagreed.
Wish you were content out in the orchards.
I'm cozy in my condo in the company
of my thoughts and the silence of a wide,
blue vista of promise.

Soulmate

What is it?
How do you recognize it?
Is it like swans who mate for life?
Are swans OK with that?
Have I had a soulmate
and not recognized him?
Daphne and Achiya say
they are each other's.
Paula and Irv were.
Christine and Denny.
Betty and Stanley.
I see too much and thus fail
at Marty's admonishment:
Don't look so hard.
Things don't bode well
in this department.

Love

You've never loved like this, Mom,
Daphne replied when I asked how many more
years she would wait for her dream man
to be free.
I haven't. Nor do I understand why a woman
continues to love a man who throws her
against a wall and cheats.
Well, that would be me re the cheat thing.
I once took back a duplicitous snake.
Till I woke up.
It's all beyond me:
Brain death by football.
The Oval Office disgrace.
War.
Smoking.
Guns.
I haven't the scintilla of a clue.

Baby Gift

Come summer, the wraps are off and the un-born,
big as pumpkins near bursting, are out on their rounds,
swimming the days away before being.
They rewind me to the sweet season I carried my own
treasure and to the sunny September Sunday
of my new life.
Who was this tiny soul whose angel face became one
with my heart and whose breath I inhaled and who
I rocked in the silent night and didn't fear for, not then,
not yet?

Heaven Sent

Up there in the infant sweepstakes,
I drew a pair of perfectly beautiful
and beautifully perfect baby girls.
We had never wanted a boy—
what would I do with a jock?

My first pink darling—Meredith.
A bright, sweet, peace-loving, graphic-designing
perfectionist Cutie; a daddy's girl, gifted enough
for equestrian blue ribbons, talented enough
for the LPGA, a yogi, a swimmer, world-class knitter,
treasured sister of Daphne, and deeply caring
and loving daughter to me.

My second little beauty—Daphne.
A feisty, wicked-clever, hilarious, candy-loving,
ageless Daffodil with the wit of a poet, writer, singer,
actor, dancer, editor, artist, healer, blogger and cook;
cherished sister of Meredith, Achiya's beloved,
and deeply caring and loving daughter to me.

In another realm, I had been someone (a Gandhi?)
or done something (twinkled the stars?)
to merit the grace and gift of these magnificent
women whose cheery *Hi, Moms* set off fireworks
of joy in my heart.
Gratitude, thy name is Lucia.

The Holy Soak

Swimming against the tide here.
I just spent $$$$ installing a tub
where there was once a mere shower.
Everyone else takes the tub out.
However. Even as my mother did,
I find the antidote to a long day's journey
is a long soak in a warm bath.

Call it hydrotherapy.
With bubbles.
And a candle.
No audiobook.
No music.
Just me and my musings.
As the book noted:
My Mother/My Self.

Gosh, Irma.
You Really Shouldn't Have

An iced latté would have sufficed
to welcome me to Sarasota Bay Club.
Nothing would do, apparently, but to put
the entire state on alert for my arrival.
A September to remember.
Schools closed.
Businesses out of business.
Planes, trains and automobiles halted.
Winds howled.
Trees swooned.
The rains forgot to stop.
Noah noah to be seen.
Very bad things happened elsewhere.
Very nice things happened here.
Our clever resident Richard screened
Singin' In The Rain.
The worst brings out the best:
The SBC staff proved in spades—
they are The Supremes.
9 a.m. Monday. A shiny new 9/11.
The Bay is less blue than grey
but the sun's out to play.
Whomever or Whatever out there
saved us, blessings.

Room Service

No calling, no waiting, no tipping.
My coffee and banana are dropped off
every morning, thanks to my thoroughly
thoughtful friend and neighbor, Irving.
Years ago, when anything went wrong
in our house in the country,
our supremely capable friend, Monroe,
came across the road and made it right.
Irving is the new Monroe.
Printer issues? TV? DVD? Sink?
Irving's your man.
Oh, and his spouse, Susie's the goddess
of the goods at Goodwill.
Need a parquet table?
An O'Keeffe cityscape?
Rose-painted chest?
Flirty skirt?
Susie's your woman.
All hail these indispensable
dispensers of wonder.
Would that we could clone them.

Breast Man

My husband was a leg man, a calling
he considered superior to the mammary variety.
I'd catch him outside the aerobics class
appraising the leaping limbs in Lycra.
He'd stare unabashedly before tending
to his own workout. A model of moderation
and discipline—never an extra ounce,
never a pat of butter or dollop of cream.
Wonder what he'd make of Roger, the lecherous
nonagenarian who makes no secret of his passion
for breasts. He is an equal-opportunity appreciator,
this Roger. He likes the small and the large,
the firm and the jiggly.
Other elders may walk with walkers and canes
or wheel about in chairs but—assuming their
marbles are relatively intact—their characters
are still in high school.
Sally is a 103-year-old wonder. Scarlet lipstick,
mischievous brown eyes, she drips with disdain
for our "president", complains over giving up
driving at 100 and plays piano jazz.
Ninety-year-old Babs displays an ankle she broke
while line dancing.
Make a note: Inside many a senior is a sophomore
looking for a party.

And another regrettable thing about death
is the ceasing of your own brand of magic
which took a whole life to develop and market.
                              - John Updike

Shelf Life

At the whizzing speed of the parade
zipping by, this is rather more than a sell-by
date; this is telling time in a warp.
Now here, now gone: my teens under a tree
reading *Seventeenth Summer.*
The numinous New York fairy tale.
My pink babies, toddlers, girls, women.
The warmth in our Marriage.
The laughter in Advertising.
My silver-free bob.
Lake Michigan out my windows.
The indelible Irma, Nina, Barbara,
Marge and Joan.
The present tense of the late USA.
This thing is on zoom.

Cold Shoulder

Working at BBDO (O being Alex Osborn
who created Brainstorming), I sat in
many a session with my fellows dreaming up
new ideas for old products.
Most notions were not to be, some survived.
Mine for Bisquick: *Impossible Pie.*

More recently, several bright souls brainstormed
innovative ideas for the fashion industry.
I've got it! one cried.
Let's cut holes in the tops of sleeves.
Brilliant! applauded another.

So here we are, people.
Throngs of women, who may or may not
have had second thoughts, are parading around
exposing full nude moons.
The subtext being...
Our truest selves include a side of lemming?
A trend has trumped taste?
I am closed if not clothes-minded?
Cut to what it is...
A new wrinkle in Urban Blight.

The United States of Amazon

This morning's headline:
Amazon will now deliver packages
to the trunk of your car.
Progress!
We can next expect the beast that Bezos
birthed to bring the box into the house,
unwrap and recycle the wrapping, pile
whatever we had to have onto the nearest pile
of whatever we had to have and fire up the Mac,
the better to Acquire whatever we have to have
from Almighty Amazon without which we
Apparently cannot survive.

Land Mines

No idea when it turned treacherous,
the landscape.
Or are you saying it's always been this way,
the terrain salted with mines?
Bob gave the Angel of Death
one hell of a run.
Sid woke up and collapsed.
Sharon choked.
You say I was too busy laughing
to notice the death part of
life-and-death?
But I am easily spooked.
Scared of the dark.
To which you say, buck up, darling?
You should have read the fine print.

Walking with the Revenants

No telling when they'll join me,
my cadre of pals who dwell elsewhere.
Marge appeared this morning, my friend
from sunny Sunday walks and talks
along the harbor.
We'd massage the issues, major and minor—
kids and partners, politics and pasta—
always finding the funny parts but never
time for the famed Philadelphia flower show.
Nina joined us, the *ne plus ultra* party-giver
with an ever-expanding Rolodex of women.
One of her parties included the publisher
who put my poems into print and launched
my career-after-the-career.
At other of her fiestas, I connected
with like-minded hearts and souls;
some for the long haul, some for short,
but all bearing gifts of insight or gossip
and amusement.

My list of chums who have dropped
off the twig grows distressingly longer.
Oh, you treasures who yet share my path,
as the hymn sings:
Abide with me; fast falls the eventide.

When the Wheels Fell Off

I'd been driving since my 15th birthday
that came with a permit license and very used
Plymouth that ferried me to and from Daddy's
butcher shop where I stood behind the counter
and sliced bologna.
And you wonder why I'm a vegetarian.
Along the road, I collected speeding tickets
thanks to a brother who taught me
to drive fast, and plenty of parking violations,
but, mercifully, no DUIs.
I learned that you stuck your hand out
to signal a left turn and up for a right.
I learned finally how to start the car
without lighting a cigarette,
how to belt up, slow down, and how to master
the exotic art of parallel parking. Not really.
I traded up to Volvos and a Hybrid that got me to
and from my give-me-this-day-my-daily Starbucks
until my eyes, my God bless them, all-observing
eyes, saw me through a trio of surgeries that culminated
in degeneration of the macular variety that has left me
car-free, if not care-free.

So it has come to pass that I now live at The Home.
Mind you, a grand home, with others who too
subscribe to Uber Alles which had nothing to do with
Nazis; it was mis-translated for propaganda.
The phrase is from an 1841 poem meaning:
more than anything. Long may it be.

Memo to Marty 2018

Here you aren't twenty-five years
after you died, or as some would say,
passed away. Uh, you *died.*
But let's consider who you would be
if you were still alive in a universe
that beggars description.
You would still be model-thin,
your beard ever trim.
Your drink still a bourbon-and-ginger ale.
Your Yiddish jokes still hilarious.
Your golf game still a struggle.
Your Ivy League threads ever perfect.
I used to tease that, because wardrobe
was your hobby, you could retire as a salesman
for Mark Shale and you'd say, *Yeah,*
and they'd pay me five bucks an hour.
Your beloved shop and all its clothes
have folded as did the mighty Marshall Field's.
I doubt you'd still be a Republican;
the party is over.
Not that the Democrats are standing tall.
Where is Bloomberg when we need him?

Once-respected figures in a host of sectors
have been outed as sexual offenders and now
decompose in a pit of disgrace.
Pity the much-maligned environment.
Pity future generations, assuming anything
in any way survives.
Nuclear war not unlikely.
We are in an appalling state.

Remember when you'd see an ancient figure
in a cruel wheelchair?
You'd look up and say,
Lord, take me before that happens.
And so He did. You, just sixty-two.
Ah, but what you've missed this
quarter of a century.

We are now really old—our friends,
my friends, and I.
Old age isn't a battle; it's a massacre.
(Philip Roth)
To wit, the relentless calls heralding
the latest assault on the latest victim.
Really, it's a tsunami, the awful news.
And it seemed to have come all in a moment.
One night we were chatting about
restaurants and vacations; the next,
it's biopsy this and hospice that.

This is my fifth memo to you.
How have I not mentioned LBGTQIA?
I've been to a lesbian wedding,
and a pair of guys in my building
were married in a synagogue.

Not that there doesn't remain vast
and vile prejudice.
And not that Roe v. Wade isn't still
and forever threatened.
As for presidents:
Black. Check.
Menace. Check.
Cue the Jew.
Hispanic.
Muslim.
Mexican.
Asian.
Gay. Maybe.
But maybe not Woman.

Trump has trumped the country
in once unimaginable ways.
I curse his image on the news and
imagine the glee of bridge players
saying No to that name in their game.

In some era, not far away, an archeologist,
assuming she has survived Zika, Ebola
and the Flu, will puzzle over moldering papers:
A driver's license? A mortgage?
What can these be, she wonders as
she leaves the house that isn't hers,
an Airbnb, she is the new homeless,
and pops into the driverless Lyft for a lift.

Hearing the siren of Thoreau to Simplify,
I sold my lovely Chicago condo overlooking
the Lake and armada of tilting sailboats.
Time for one house, not two.
Not without pangs did I abandon
a half-century of friends and memories.
I have left a life before.
When a mystical hand at my back
nudged me into the corner office to resign,
I was a mere fifty and had nothing left
to give crazy marvelous crazy Advertising.
My thirty-year war over, I segued
into a freelance career that ended
as your pancreatic cancer began.
You, the poster boy for health and fitness,
would be dead in two years.
And I, at fifty-seven, would become,
as you called me: The Widow Blinn.
Dating, God help me; not that He did,
considering the mostly sorry roster.
I am best off a solo.

MFK Fisher wrote about her much-loved
last house in Sonoma.
Unless Mr. Darcy rides up and whisks me away
to Pemberley, I am ensconced in my last house,
a cozy nest overlooking Sarasota Bay
where I live among those who, like me,
have had to give up their cars.
It happened in a blur, the car thing.
As Capote put it:
Life is a moderately good play
with a badly written third act.

Incredibly, I am in my eighties,
marbles relatively intact, ten years
beyond my mother. Granted another ten,
she would have continued her stations of the cross:
washing/ironing/cooking/cleaning/worry.
My life, immeasurably larger, mirrors hers in fear.
A woman of few words, she forewarned:
You will worry about your children
for the rest of your life.

The future winks.
Come, pack lightly.

About the Author

Lucia Blinn, storyteller/poet/former New York/Chicago advertising writer, lives in Sarasota, FL and shares her witty stories at readings everywhere.

luciablinn@gmail.com